MW01236089

BROKEN

Is This My Reality?

Rosalyn D. Smith

Trilogy Christian Publishers

A Wholly Owned Subsidiary of Trinity Broadcasting Network

2442 Michelle Drive

Tustin, CA 92780

Copyright © 2021 by Rosalyn Smith

For information, address Trilogy Christian Publishing

Rights Department, 2442 Michelle Drive, Tustin, Ca 92780.

Trilogy Christian Publishing/ TBN and colophon are trademarks of Trinity Broadcasting Network.

For information about special discounts for bulk purchases, please contact Trilogy Christian Publishing.

Manufactured in the United States of America

Trilogy Disclaimer: The views and content expressed in this book are those of the author and may not necessarily reflect the views and doctrine of Trilogy Christian Publishing or the Trinity Broadcasting Network.

10 9 8 7 6 5 4 3 2 1

Library of Congress Cataloging-in-Publication Data is available.

ISBN 978-1-63769-008-6

ISBN 978-1-63769-009-3 (ebook)

INTRODUCTION

Hannah is the editor of her school yearbook. She is active in several clubs at school and is known to others as the "good girl." She and her friends have finally made it to their senior year when the worst of what they can imagine happens. Hannah's best friend's mom passes, which makes her friend look at herself while confronting suicide. Hannah's boyfriend turns controlling, and she learns that he is better at helping his friends out than at making good decisions with her. The stress of everything ends up with Hannah's summer being hit with the unthinkable, all while her Christianity is challenged. Is she dreaming, or is this her life's reality?

DEDICATION

I dedicate this book to my family who is always patient with me while I am working long hours. They realize my life belongs to the Lord and that we were all born with a purpose. I also want to dedicate this book to my mother, a single parent, who always made sure my sister and I did not lack for any good thing when growing up. Finally, to my grandmother who is resting in heaven, I am who I am today because of her prayers, faithfulness, dedication, and love of Christ. I am Blessed!

CONTENTS

DISBELIEF

CHAPTER 1

"Jesus, forgive me!" I lay there in a trance, not believing I had carried it out. It was over. I had actually done it. My seventeen-year-old body couldn't move—all I could do was think, *What have I done?* I think my loud scream scared the nurse and the doctor who had completed the procedure. They glanced at each other, then they looked at me as if they were frightened interns who had made a mistake. The nurse said softly, "Let me help you up."

As I stood up, I noticed on the floor a white container that was covered up. I could not see the contents clearly, but I saw the shape of what was inside. It scared me to no end, and I began to feel sick, because what was inside was very tiny and helpless. I got dressed and was escorted to a recovery room for about ten minutes. I was in disbelief at what had just occurred. I sat for what felt like an eternity. All I could think about was the white container on the floor and what I had done. I was given a grief brochure and a business card with a counseling hotline number to call if I needed to talk to someone. Another lady then told me that I was free to leave when my ten minutes were up, and to take care of myself. I thanked her and walked toward the door that was in the back of the building. As I looked back at the nurse, I saw another girl sitting, looking sad and upset just like me. I closed the door behind me, and the tears began to fall as I walked to the car.

The ride home with Steven was quiet—so much so that we could hear the heat sizzling on the hot southern road. While he was driving, I could also hear the warm, roaring wind hitting my face. It felt like we were strangers in a crowded car. Neither of us wanted to confront what we had done. How could we be so careless, stupid, and selfish? As we arrived at my house from the thirty-minute drive that felt like an hour, the water sprinklers circled in a perfect motion on the lawn. The car stopped in front of my two-story brick home. I could see that I had not opened my blinds this morning, because I was so anxious to leave my house. I didn't want to arrive to a bright, happy room. The darkness in the room would fit how I was feeling.

Steven touched my hand, then my chin, moving my face toward his direction. He wiped the one tear that hadn't blown away in the wind as he drove his convertible black Mustang. He said, "I love you and will always love you; please call me when you feel better. Just remember, we will get through this."

I had no words, only regret that we had ever met. I grabbed my Nike satchel and slammed his car door. As I walked toward the back of my house to the kitchen door entrance, my only thought was that I didn't want to see my mother. But guess who greeted me at the door—my mom.

"Hi, Honey! How was your run with Steven?"

"Hi, Mom," I replied with disgust.

"What's wrong—did you two have an argument?"

"No, ma'am! I just started my period, and I don't feel so good."

"Oh, you poor thing. Well, I was thinking it was that time, so when I went shopping early this morning I picked you up some extra feminine products and Tylenol. I placed them in your bathroom."

In a sarcastic voice I replied, "Thanks, Mom! You always know what I need!"

"Moms always know what their children need!" She walked over to me with her shades on and gave me a kiss on my cheek, and continued with, "Jackie and I are having lunch together, so I will see you later."

Jackie and my mom were old college friends. They tried to have lunch once a month if they could, but I could have sworn they were together two weeks ago. It didn't really matter; I was just happy she would not be at home. I didn't feel like catering to all of her questions. Since my dad was out of town with my brother Julius at a football camp, I knew we would have to entertain each other. I was not in the mood to talk to anyone—not Mom, and not even my best friend Cassandra, who thankfully was out of town.

"Bye, Mom, see you later."

What did her comment mean: "Moms always know what their children need"? She had always said that moms know everything, but this time it sounded different. Was it me and my paranoia, or did she know what I had experienced this morning? I thought, *No!* I was just beginning to panic. I headed upstairs to my bedroom, cleaned up, took two Tylenol and placed the bottle on my nightstand, grabbed my teddy bear that my daddy had given me when I was three, and slid under my covers for a long nap, hoping, wishing, and praying that when I woke up I would just be experiencing an awful dream that even I could not have made up.

TRUTH

CHAPTER 2

"Good morning, sweet girl!"

My eyes popped open with fear, because I was still in a deep sleep. It was 7:00 a.m. on Sunday morning. I couldn't believe I had slept from 1:00 p.m. until now. OMG, I didn't even remember dreaming. However, I did remember getting up to use the bathroom around 12:00 a.m., only because I had looked at my cell phone to see if I had a text from that no-good, conniving boyfriend. I only remembered crawling back into my bed for more sleep.

"Good morning, Mom! How long have you been standing there?"

"Just for a few minutes. I wanted to check on you since you have slept all night. How are you feeling today, any better?"

It was then that my mom reminded me that I was not in an awful dream. What I had gone through yesterday was truly my life's reality.

"I still have a few cramps. Do you mind if I stay home from church today?"

"Sure, I think that is a good idea. Read some of the Bible, pray, and you can even catch the service on the internet. I will pick up something for dinner—not sure if I feel like doing much cooking today. I expect Dad and Julius to return this evening, so I will grab something for all of us. Please take a good shower so you feel better, and take two more of those extra strength Tylenol."

"Thank you so much, Mom! That sounds like a good plan. Enjoy the service at church."

Mom walked away with a sad disposition. I was not sure what was bothering her, but I could tell it was something. She always cooked on Sunday, especially if Dad had been away. She wanted him to have a good, nutritious meal after all the fast food that he had probably consumed with Julius.

Part of me did not want to be alone, because I didn't want to think about my terrible sin. However, the other part of me didn't want to talk to anyone. I had to deal with my sin on my own; at least, that is what I thought.

After my shower, I put on some fresh PJs and headed to the kitchen. The house was so clean, as if it had never been lived in. When Lil' J (that is what I called Julius) was not home, the house seemed so peaceful and calm.

I poured some orange juice and ate a Danish, just to add a little sugar in my system from all the blood I had lost. I wasn't even hungry—just feeling heartbroken and very sore.

I cleaned up my breakfast and washed my two dish items. Mom had the house so clean, I hated to leave even a crumb on the counter.

As I returned to my bedroom, I slithered back into my bed. Then I got out of bed, trying to decide if I should fall to my knees and pray. *Why should I*, I thought. *I am probably destined for hell. My life is over, and I am just a walking sinner with no hope.* I decided to get back in the bed. I knew that the Good Lord didn't want to hear anything I had to say. I picked up my cell phone to see if I had any text messages. I didn't. I began to feel even more foolish. He didn't even have the decency to text me to see how I was doing. How thoughtless of him. The tears began to fall, and I tried not to cry, but I could not keep my composure. I picked up my laptop that was next to me in my bed, and I logged in to watch the service at my church. I was wondering if I could spot my mom in the large congregation. Looking at my mom would at least give me some comfort—she always knew what to do. If the Lord didn't forgive me, I didn't know how I could ever forgive myself. I knew I needed to try not to hate Steven. It took both of us to make a decision as sad and as final as the one we had made yesterday.

"God loves you, and there is nothing you can do about it!" That is what I heard Pastor Ronnie say as I tuned in.

"Wow, what timing—he just started preaching."

"My sermon today is titled, 'God's Love Saves'!" He went on to say, "Regardless of where we are in our life, regardless of what we may be doing or have done, God loves us, and He wants us to live eternal life with Him. All we have to do is acknowledge that Jesus is the Son of God."

He went on to quote verses from the Bible and tell funny stories about how we think everything is tragic in our lives. If he only knew that real tragedy really existed! I was experiencing it right now!

He then quoted, "If we confess our sins, God is faithful and just to forgive us of our sins and to cleanse us from all unrighteousness, because John 3:16 in the King James says, 'For God so loved the world, that he gave his only begotten Son, that whosoever believeth in him should not perish, but have everlasting life.' So, enter through the door of salvation and repent of your sins. Every day is a new day, so again, I say, repent!

God's mercy and grace will be with you—all you have to do is ask for forgiveness every time, and as many times as needed. You may make mistake after mistake, but please do not give up, cave in, or quit. Each day you will get better and become more knowledgeable of how God wants you to live. God forgives and will save us—all we simply have to do is ask Him to!"

One of my good male friends has always reminded me that he doesn't believe in God. He has always asked me how I can believe in a man that I cannot see. I then would remind him that I would rather believe in God than not. If I believe in Him, then I have a chance to spend eternity with Him. If He is not real, then I guess I will spend eternity somewhere else, but at least believing in Him will not hurt my chances of spending eternity somewhere else if He isn't real. So, why not put all my hope and trust in God while I'm living on this earth? Plus, He is a God of love, peace, and joy. Too bad I was not a representative of God, like I had thought. If I was, I would not do things that make Him unhappy.

I shouted, as if Pastor Ronnie could hear me, "How can God love me? I am so stupid! I grew up in the church! I know right from wrong, but I failed Him! I failed myself, my parents, and those who depended or could have depended on me!"

I pondered and pondered and still believed that I was a disappointment, a failure, and a lost cause. It was a great message from Pastor Ronnie, and I was glad I had caught some of it. However, my heart was so broken that I couldn't imagine it ever mending.

I prayed and then cried myself to sleep. I was so glad that I had drifted off into a restorative stage of sleep—it was there that I couldn't feel any pain.

I dreamt of driving to a green meadow. I got out of the car, and there were the prettiest flowers that I had ever seen. I ran to smell the flowers, and I even started laughing in my dream. It was peaceful, I felt free, I felt safe—but most importantly, I felt happy. But then, at the end of the dream I saw that white container again, and it was as if someone was trying to take the cover off for me to see what was inside; then I woke up.

COMFORT

CHAPTER 3

"Wake up, wake up! Have you been sleeping the entire time I've been gone?"

"Hey, little stinker! When did you and Dad get back?"

Lil' J replied, "Last night, around 7:00 p.m., but you were sleeping with your mouth wide open and your tongue hanging out."

Julius was laughing so hard that I began to laugh. He went on to say, "Mom and Dad both were checking on you as if you had no pulse. What is wrong with you? Did you miss your favorite brother so much that you just slept until I returned?"

"Funny little man! No, and you are my only brother! I was not feeling well yesterday, so I had to sleep it off. I didn't even realize you were gone, but I did realize all the peace and relaxation I was getting while you were away! It was nice not hearing your ridiculous jokes and your whiny little voice all the time!"

"Well," Julius replied, until Mom cut him off.

"Could you two please stop irritating each other? I am headed to work, so try and have a good day!" my mother shouted, as she passed by my bedroom door.

Mom was a high school counselor. She worked so hard, and with school starting soon, she was meeting with new students and finalizing school schedules before the start of the school year. This was her busy time, as she always told us. Which meant find your own dinner, or eat leftovers.

"Bye, Mom!" we both shouted.

"How was your trip, Lil' J?"

I was only playing with Julius. I loved him dearly, and I actually had missed him. He made me laugh, and he was a really good little brother. I was so happy he would be with me in high school during my senior year.

He went on to tell me about his adventure at a D1 football camp. It brought me joy to see him so happy. So much so that my eyes began to water with excitement for him. I didn't even realize it, but a few tears fell down my cheek.

"Okay, this is weird—why are you crying about me talking about football?" he asked.

I replied, "I'm not crying. In the morning, my eyes are sensitive to light and my eyes drain from it. Before falling asleep, I didn't close my window blinds, so that maybe why you see a tear or two." Just then, we both realized my blinds were still closed.

Julius gave me a puzzled look with a crazy smile as he walked toward the door. I finished the conversation as he walked away by saying, "Glad you and Dad made it back safely."

My bedroom went from laughter to complete silence. I didn't realize I had slept all night again. Mom didn't even wake me for dinner. What was wrong with me—was I becoming depressed? All I knew was that I felt a little better. However, I was still cramping and very sore. I didn't want to get out the bed; all I wanted to do was lie on my back and look at the ceiling and not think about my life. How could I erase this lingering pain in my bleeding heart?

I attempted to read Philippians 4:13 (KJV), "*I can do all things through Christ which strengtheneth me.*" That scripture had always put things in perspective for me, but I normally read it when I had an editing deadline for the yearbook at school, or when I was working on an assignment that I was struggling with. But now the words meant so much more to me. I now realized that what I had done was wrong. God would have met me where I was. He would have made sure I had everything I needed to deal with a situation that I had made final. It was then that I closed my bedroom door, fell to my knees, and cried out to my God. I asked for forgiveness; I prayed then I cried; I cried then I prayed. I asked the Lord to forgive me again and again for not trusting Him to take care of me. I knew I had failed Him. I lay back down in my bed until I stopped crying. I was scared, alone, and had no clue what to do with my life. I was so broken. I drifted off to sleep for a few minutes. I dreamt about those beautiful flowers again. They had colors that my eyes had never witnessed before. They were so pretty, and all I could do was run up to them and smell the sweet smell that they gave. I could feel myself smiling as I was dreaming and running through the beautiful field of flowers.

PEACE

CHAPTER 4

I decided to get up. I showered, washed some clothes, changed my sheets, and even got dressed and opened my blinds. Then I realized this was the last week of summer break—how terrible. I didn't want to go back to school; I was only looking forward to graduation and going to college. I started thinking that once I got away from this city, maybe I could forget about some folks here, and the drama. I tried to leave my room, but I couldn't. I crawled on top of my neatly made-up bed. It was my safe place. It was comfortable, and no one was in my room to judge me. I felt sad, depressed, and lonely. I felt as if I shouldn't be excited about graduation, college, or anything else that pertained to life. I didn't even want to eat breakfast. I didn't want to talk to anyone; I didn't even want to check my phone to look at TikTok, Snapchat, Instagram, or even my text messages. Looking at all those happy faces wasn't something I wanted to see. Everyone and their perfect life. All I could think about was my life. Sleeping felt so much better. It was peaceful, relaxing, and energizing to a certain degree. Another plus with sleep is that I could avoid thinking about what I had done, because dreaming about those beautiful flowers was better than my life's reality—until that awful container would show up in my dream, and then I would wake up.

All of a sudden, I remembered Pastor Ronnie's message from yesterday, so I began to repent, yet again. Then I cried as I began to pray,

"Lord, I know I may not be one of your favorite people right now, but my heart is heavy. Please know that if I could go back in time, the outcome would be different. Lord, show me how I can ease the pain that I feel. I am so sorry, Lord. My heart hurts; I don't want to live, because I am not fit to love others. Help me, in Jesus' name, amen!"

I drank the glass of orange juice my little brother had left on my nightstand when I was in the shower. He even wrote a note. It read, "I'm headed to football practice, hope you are feeling better. Lil' J."

He was such a sweetheart. Then I thought, "Lord, thank you for my family!"

I fell back to sleep, but this time I only slept for three hours, because I heard Julius and Cassandra coming into the house, singing and stomping up the stairs—then they busted through my bedroom door like wild children and started jumping on my bed. Lil' J ran to his room to take a shower after singing with San for a few minutes.

"Wake up, get up, and let's go!" shouted Cassandra, while laughing. "Why are you in this bed?" she asked.

"Hi, San," (that is what I call her). We gave each other a big hug. San had been in a treatment facility for over a month. "I thought you were coming home later this week—when did you get here?"

"My dad and grandma picked me up yesterday."

"It is so good to see you. How are you doing?" I asked. San had watched her mom die in the hospital a few months ago. She became depressed and started having anxiety attacks.

She would not talk to anyone about her grief except me and my mom. Then one day, at her home, she attempted suicide. She was missing her mom so much, and had even begun to feel guilty for her death. San's dad had realized that he could not help her. We had all realized that a month after her mom's death, she had begun cutting herself; she had said it was a way to relieve her pain. I was so upset with her when I saw all the cuts on her legs that I immediately told my mom, who then called her dad. I had also told her to use some ice when she felt like wanting to cut—at least she would get a numbing sensation instead of the ugly cuts, which were dangerous. I had read that tip in one of my mom's mental counseling magazines.

My mom had given San's dad a list of treatment facilities that could assist with San's needs. However, he never said anything to her about the cuts until she overdosed on some sleeping pills. I was so glad she hadn't ended her life. She was spunky, smart, and full of life. She was a good friend, one that had so much to offer life, and one I really needed right now.

"I am better, I guess," San replied. "I have had individual and group counseling, I have set goals, and I have been evaluated and medicated—I have refused to keep taking meds. I didn't like feeling like a zombie. I told all the doctors that I was ready for what life wanted to throw my way. I will have grief counseling with a group twice a month, and individual counseling with my therapist once a month at least, until they see progress. They did their best to help me, but I will always miss my mom and have regret for some of the awful things I said to her. I love and miss her so much. I write in a journal to her, even though she cannot read it. It is what helps me."

"Well, you look great! You are right, you will always miss your mom. It is just knowing what to do when you start missing her. You know we are here for you if you need anything! I'm just so happy you are back! I love you, San!"

We continued to talk about her treatment and the steps she must take when she got in a sad and lonely place. All I could do was think about how strong she was in front of me. She had lost her mom, and she had tried to take on her mom's role by taking care of her grandmother, who had moved in with the family two years ago. San was under so much stress that she had cracked under pressure while trying to maintain a perfect 4.0 GPA.

Her dad had realized how much Cassandra was trying to be the perfect daughter. She would cook for the family while her mom was going through cancer treatments. She cleaned the house, ran errands, and studied until all hours of the night. I became stressed just watching her do all of this.

Mom and I would take Sunday dinner to the family, and we would sit with her grandmother when San and her dad were at the hospital visiting with her mother. My mom knew it was a lot on everyone in the Davis family. She had even invited Grandma Davis over to our house to spend a few days with us after the death of Mrs. Davis, allowing San and her dad a chance to mourn and to clean out her things. The reality that her mom was no longer in the house was too much for San. After she took some extra pills to get some rest one night, she ran to her dad's room crying, with the empty bottle in her hand, and collapsed. He called 911, my mom, and his sister. When they were at the hospital, the doctor said that if San hadn't immediately run to her dad she wouldn't be here with us today. The doctor had also told her that she was one of the lucky ones, but I called her one of the blessed ones, because I saw blessings when she talked and interacted with others. She was so special, and I let her know it every time we were together.

Cassandra and I had talked so much that we began to finally sit in silence. We lay across my bed, and then I held San's hand and prayed with her. I didn't care how she felt about it or what she would think, but I prayed with her,

"Heavenly Father, thank you for my best friend Cassandra. Thank you for placing her around those who have her best interests at heart. Thank you for her mental strength and her ability to look to you for strength, joy, and happiness. Thank you for showing her how to carry on. In the Bible it says that you will keep us in perfect peace, and that you will strengthen and keep us. Thank you in advance for keeping your word. These things I pray, in Jesus' name, amen."

San smiled at me with tears flowing down her face, and she said, "Thank you, best friend."

It was then that I realized that praying for someone else had helped me with my painful reality. I began to feel peace come over me.

HEALING

CHAPTER 5

San and I decided to go grab something to eat. We went to this new pizzeria close to home. I didn't have much of an appetite, but I realized I hadn't eaten anything solid in about two days. We shared a pizza and ordered individual side salads. It was nice getting out of the house and getting some fresh air. While we were eating, San asked me why I had prayed for her. I told her that I hadn't thought about it—I just knew that prayer made me feel better when I was down and needed strength. I told her she was like a sister to me, and that is how I was raised. It was important for family to pray for each other. San stopped eating and told me that no other friend of hers had ever prayed for her out loud, except for her mother and grandmothers. She thanked me again as she shed a few tears.

At that moment, it felt as if San and I had reached a new level of friendship and respect for each other. I felt her pain and understood what she was going through. The loss that she was experiencing was real. The separation of mother and child was something that she would have to adjust to. I reminded her that she had several memories of her mother, even her mother's touch and her sweet smell. I reminded San that some mothers and their children never got to experience those moments due to tragedy or unexpected loss. I also reminded San that God would be with her, and all she had to do was open up to Him in prayer and never hesitate to talk to Him, like we had done for the last five hours. We finished what we could, and I asked her to take the pizza home to her dad. The one piece I'd had was enough for me, and I told her that Lil' J would be forced to eat a home-cooked meal tonight because of all the fast food he had eaten this past weekend.

As San drove me home, the pain in my heart still ached, but I realized that the darkness that was hanging over me was only for a moment. The prayer and conversations with San gave me hope for continuing on. I wasn't ready to share with her what I was going through. This was her moment to heal. While she was healing, I was touched at the same time and could tell life would still go on for me.

San and I said goodnight as she pulled up to my house. I told her to text me when she arrived home, even though she lived one street over. We always told the other one to text when arriving home. As I walked to my front door, my dad opened it and said, "Hey, Buttons" to me and waved bye to Cassandra.

Dad asked me how San was doing, and I told him she seemed to be doing really well, considering everything. I told him about our day, and he smiled and replied, "The gifts within you are starting to rise up. Continue having a voice that stands strong for Christ and see your rewards begin to be uncovered."

My dad was so dramatic at times. He meant well. I laughed at him and said goodnight to both parents. I still didn't want to answer questions or have a long conversation with them, so I headed to my room for bed.

Steven's Reality

PETRIFIED

CHAPTER 6

I thought this couldn't happen the first time! This locker room talk was full of bull! Why did I listen to Matthew? I thought he was supposed to be my boy! He said girls can't get pregnant the first time. I punched a hole in my bedroom wall as I thought more about what Hannah was sharing with me on the phone. She said she was two weeks. She told me she went to a family planning center to get a blood test while dressed in a disguise. She went on to say that the nurse told her she was pregnant.

I fell to the floor next to my bed as she continued to talk. I told her that I was sorry this had happened, but in no way could I raise a child, and that I was not going to let my mom, my grandma, and even my dad down. Even though my dad died overseas in the war years ago, I did not want to put his name to shame by having a child out of wedlock.

"Hannah, you know I love you and will do anything for you, but I can't do this! We cannot have this child. I cannot be the person for it that I know I should be! I cannot and will not ask my mom to help support a child. I haven't even graduated from high school yet. I cannot and will not do this. I will pay for a procedure to be done and we can move on, but just know that I cannot and will not be a part of this. This is too much! I am just now dealing with my dad's death and not having him around. Let's take care of this soon; I will pay for anything you need. I have more than enough money in my savings to get whatever you need and will take care of everything. I am done talking about this for now. I must take my little sister to dance for my mom. I will call you later. Don't worry about it—I will take care of it, you just relax."

I hung up my cell phone, not giving her another opportunity to talk. I didn't want to hear another word come out of her mouth regarding this subject. I had plans—big plans, to be exact. I had three colleges wanting me to play QB at their school. What would I look like as a quarterback with a child? I knew she would want me to marry her, since they were these "big-time Christians" walking around town. I didn't want to hear her dad's voice, and I surely didn't want to answer to her mom, who was my high school counselor. They were good people, but I never said that I would marry their daughter—I was not ready for this! If I didn't play in college, I could even get an academic scholarship with my grades and college entrance exams. Plus, how many athletes participate in the Student Government Association… not many! I had so much to offer others, but not to a child—not yet!

I sat there for about thirty minutes, until Tiffany reminded me that we needed to leave for her dance lessons. I grabbed my keys, and I purposely left my cell phone on my bed. This felt like a terrible nightmare that I could not escape from. The only way I thought I could escape from this unbelief was by leaving my cell phone at home. I did not want to see any messages from Hannah or her parents, so I left it under my pillow, on silent.

DECEITFUL

CHAPTER 7

"Hannah, stop crying, before your mom hears you! I understand you don't want to do this. Since you don't want to have the procedure, tell me how you will take care of a baby your senior year? Who will be there when you are in school and your parents are working? Who will care for the child when you are studying late at night? You will be the talk of the town, at church and at school. Just relax by getting some sleep. I'm just glad you discovered this early. I made a withdrawal today after calling around to see how much this would cost. I love you, and I will pick you up Saturday morning at 7:30 a.m. Just tell your mom that we are taking a jog in the morning at the city trails, like we used to do. Try and have a good night."

Hannah was sweet, innocent, and compassionate, but very naive. I was the best person for her. I knew how to talk sense into her. She had her entire life ahead of her. She would thank me for this later.

After eating dinner and taking a shower, I told my mom that I was headed to bed so that I could enjoy an early jog in the morning with Hannah. Next thing I knew, my mom wanted to play one hundred questions by asking me how Hannah and I were doing and if she was the girl for me. She even asked what my plans were after we graduated, and if we were going to continue dating. I answered what I could, but I said with a laugh, "Mom, chill with all the questions." She smiled, kissed me on my cheek, and said she loved me. She was acting very weird, but I kissed her back and headed to bed.

I tried to sleep, but I was very restless. All I could think about was how Hannah was doing. I tried to put myself in her shoes. I knew she was scared and very upset about this entire thing. I started to feel like it was my fault. This was not supposed to happen, but one thing had led to another that night. Hannah said it had happened so quickly that she didn't realize the intimacy we had shared was happening until it did. I honestly didn't think she would get pregnant. I knew we had dated for over a year, and I had been patient—I tried not to bring up sex, even though it crossed my mind. Hannah was special, and I wanted our first time together to be special, even though she was practicing celibacy until marriage. I think that night we both were in the moment, and our passion got in the way. She was upset that I was spending more time with my friends and not with her like I used to. I was comforting her, and one thing had led to another.

Since I couldn't sleep, I texted Hannah that I loved her and that I would be there for her always. I also told her that I would be with her the entire time tomorrow. I ended with how smart she was and that she was doing what was best for everyone, including herself. She didn't respond, but I felt better. I got over my guilt and finally fell asleep.

FORSAKEN

CHAPTER 8

I was so nervous driving to Hannah's house that the hair on my head was dripping with sweat. I was driving so fast that I didn't even remember driving; I was in a daze. What was wrong with me? I stopped at the four way stop for five minutes to gather myself. Once I felt like Steven, I pulled up to Hannah's house. I was so thankful that she saw me from her bedroom window and came outside. It was 7:30 a.m., and I had a thirty-minute drive ahead of me.

"Good morning," I said. I couldn't think of anything else that made sense at that moment.

I turned the radio off, just in case she wanted to talk about what was about to happen, but she didn't say a word, not even good morning. I could tell she had been crying. Hannah had on her Ray-Ban sunglasses with no makeup on, and her hair was up in a ball. As I looked at the side of her left eye, it looked puffy—she looked nothing like my sweet Hannah. She had her Nike gear on, with a hat over her hair. I guess we were both trying to disguise our look with a hat and shades.

Fifteen minutes had gone by, and we still were not talking.

I finally said, "Hannah, talk to me. We always talk—you are one of my best friends, and it doesn't feel right not talking. What's on your mind?" I didn't really mean to ask what was on her mind—of course I knew that answer, and how I regret asking that question. She was furious!

"How dare you ask me what is on my mind! You know what is on my mind, and it is not doing this! You shared your heart and true concerns regarding how you feel, and I shared mine! Don't ask me how I'm doing, or what I'm thinking, or anything, unless you turn this car around and we talk to our parents about what to do!"

That fifteen minutes turned into another fifteen minutes, and I realized I had parked my car. I sat in silence for five minutes after she went off on me. I had no words, only regret that she was so upset.

"Hannah, we are here. I cannot turn this car around, but I do respect the fact that you do not want to do this. I cannot force you to go inside, but please know how I feel about the entire situation. I read that it is a fast procedure, and I promise I will be here for you. Here is an extra wallet with several hundred dollars. Use what you need, and keep the rest for what you may be in need of after it's done. Please know that I am so sorry about this entire situation. I love you!"

"Stop talking! I can't hear any more lies! Stay in the car. I will text you when I am ready! I will do this alone!"

She snatched the wallet and slammed my door. All I could do was notice the girls that were walking in. Some with their moms, some with I guess boyfriends, and others alone, like Hannah. As she walked away, I suddenly became sick. I drove to a store and got some Gatorade. I drove back, parked my car, said a prayer for Hannah, and took a nap until I got my text.

REGRET

CHAPTER 9

Hannah looked sick as she approached my car. I didn't know what to say. She sat in the car and cried all the way to her house. Hannah cried so much that I started crying. I apologized to her, to God, and to myself for letting everyone down. What was I to do? I had never done this, and I prayed I would never have to again. I felt the pain that was coming from her heart—it was as if someone had abandoned her and left her alone. I guess I had—not a good feeling. I had never witnessed her in this state before, so I pulled over by a park a block away from her house, in order for her to get her composure before we arrived at her house. Hannah finally stopped crying. I didn't know what to say; I just stared as she wiped her face. We finally arrived at her house. I asked if I could walk her in; however, she threw my wallet back at me, got out of my car, slammed the door, and ran toward the back of the house. Thankfully, I was able to tell her that I loved her and that we would get through this together before she vanished. I also told her that I would call when she felt better.

When I arrived home, I just wanted to be alone. The guilt of what I had asked Hannah to do was really working on me. How could I be the man of my mom's house and a leader on the field, but a boy when it came to adult responsibilities that concerned my life and the life of those that I could have loved?

I needed some time to think and clear my head, so I decided to drive two hours away to our family beach home, since no one was renting it for the weekend. I told my mom I was going to work on some football plays and needed to regroup.

I picked up two of my friends who also played football. They were cool dudes that I enjoyed hanging around. When we arrived, we all decided we would eat, chill for a little, and then hit the sand in order to work on drills to better prepare for Monday's practice at noon.

This was what I needed! The water, the sand, nice warm air, and no girl going off on me. I needed to think and hang with my boys. Little did I know that it would turn into a party weekend.

"Matthew and Nathan, how could you invite all these girls to come hang with us? We are supposed to get our workout going this weekend!"

"I know, Steven, but Tonya Walker and her friends were available to come hang out. They will be here around 7:00 p.m. So, we have plenty of time to practice. You have been acting stressed, and I know I'm stressed out from those coaches who have worked my last nerves. Who cares that I am not as big as they want me to be? Who can gain twenty pounds over the summer? Man, they have been messing with my head. I should sue them all for child endangerment."

We all laughed at Nathan.

"But seriously, those coaches don't care anything about us. They treat us like slaves in the way they talk to us. All they want is a win. They don't take the time to really get to know us. I have absolutely no respect for them, and regret that I ever met them. They say they want to make us stronger and better, but they want me to quit or be the water boy, as the head coach said one day. He was not joking! They will remember me, because I will do great things in life. If not in sports, then in business. They all have sons, and one day someone will treat their sons the same way they have been treating me, and all the other players that don't look the way they want them to look. I am really hating them the more I think about it, but as my grandma would always say, vengeance is the Lord's; He will repay those who do his children wrong and unfairly. He knows how to take a bad situation and turn it around for our good, and I believe my granny!"

We let Nathan vent, but he was speaking truth. The coaches were harder on him and others they really didn't want on the field. It was like they didn't know how to bring greatness out of players that didn't fit their circle of athletes. They expected them to already come in knowing everything, and that was not good coaching. I felt for my friend, because he was a good kid. I didn't want him to think he was any less than anyone else; that was why I took time to work with him, and that's why I had brought him on this trip: he was really a good player. He was just not from the privileged side of town, and his dad was not dishing out several hundreds of dollar bills weekly for him to get a starting position, like some on the team.

"Nathan, don't hate—I know you are speaking out of anger. However, we have been together for four years, so let's end our senior year with a bang and learn not to act like those careless coaches who only take interest in players that are twenty pounds overweight and too fat to run on the field. Players in our class have been faithful, patient, and hardworking, and have never lost a game in three years. Like you said, vengeance is the Lord's, and I can't wait for them to realize you don't treat your players wrong. With that being said, let's hit the sand for some workouts before these girls drop in. I need to go to the store and get snacks for our pretty guests, and you party animals are going to help chip in on the food."

"Sounds good to me, fellas! Let's hit it so that we can have some fun, food, and females—this is my kind of weekend," Matthew said with a smile.

Matthew had told me last week he needed to get away. His older brother had been incarcerated for two years now for a crime that was senseless. This had taken a toll on him and his mom, who was a single parent. Matthew's brother, Miguel, was at the wrong place at the wrong time, and with the wrong people. His mom didn't have enough money to bail him out, let alone get a lawyer to represent him. He told me he prayed for his brother daily, but he felt like his prayers were not getting answered. I just told him to keep praying that God would surround his brother with some good people while in jail until his trial, and to pray that favor would overtake him, because he didn't deserve to be in that awful place. We could only hope that God was listening.

"All right, it's on! Let's hit the sand, men!" We all ran out to the beach with our footballs, water, and cleats. *This is exactly what I needed,* I thought, as I was running to the sand. *A nice weekend away from it all.*

Cassandra's Reality

DEPARTURE

CHAPTER 10

"Mom, don't go! I need you! Please don't leave me! I love you, and I am so sorry!"

I couldn't believe I had watched my mom take her last breath. I had been so mean to her. She had wanted to be my best friend during my teen years, but I was ashamed of her. Now that she was lying in the bed, I saw how strong and beautiful she was. She loved me so much! She wanted me to be the best at everything I did. She worked so hard to make sure I had everything I needed, and all I could do was complain.

"She is gone, Cassandra! She knew you loved her, and she loved you more than life itself! Let's allow the nurses to take care of her. We should give her another kiss and say our last goodbyes."

I gave Mom a kiss, and Dad kissed her like she was a delicate rose; it even made the nurses' eyes water, the way he kissed her. He then said a prayer and whispered in her ear, "We will see each other again, my Angel; rest well! I love you!"

My dad grabbed my hand, and we walked out the door. I couldn't walk away without looking back at my sweet mom. When she was out of my sight, the tears rushed out of my eyes like a river. This was so final. How did this happen to my family? As I looked at my dad, he was so strong. You could tell that he had been crying, but he walked away with such confidence that we would be okay.

When we got home, Hannah and her mom were still at our house. They were with my grandmother, who lived with us. My dad had called Mrs. Myers to inform her that my mother had passed away. They were so sweet—they had cooked dinner for my grandmother, cleaned our house, and even washed a few of our clothes. I loved my best friend Hannah and her mom; at times, I think I treated Mrs. Myers better than I treated my mom.

After the Myers left, and my grandmother went to bed, my dad and I talked about my mom and the cancer that had lived in her body. My mom had been living with pancreatic cancer for the last four years. She was diagnosed when I was thirteen. The doctors said that she was one of their healthiest patients who had fought the hardest. My dad shared with me how the two of them had talked about this day, and what life would be like without her. Dad said that last week, Mom had known it was a matter of days before she was going to go to heaven. He said that was why he couldn't cry much, simply because they had cried together for years. They had finally realized that they wanted to live, laugh, and love as long as they could, with each other and with me. However, I told Dad that I was an awful daughter, and that I had finally come around just a few months ago, but through it all Mom had kept a smile on her face and loved me anyway. The more I thought about my behavior, the more sorrowful I became. My dad held me half the night as I cried. When I drifted off to sleep, Dad lay me in my mom's favorite beige chaise lounge chair in their room, covered me with her sweet-smelling fleece blanket, and let me sleep, like he did when I was a little girl.

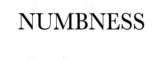

NUMBNESS

CHAPTER 11

The funeral was very nice. It amazed me that Mom had picked out her clothes, the music, who would speak, even her favorite Bible scriptures that would be read. Mom had even ordered Dad roses to be delivered to the house the morning of the funeral, with a very loving message. She had called the florist and asked if she could please help her honor and celebrate her best friend when she departed this earth. Dad said she had done everything with the exception of picking out her casket; it was too much for her to think about while living. He said planning the funeral was like planning a party, since she loved to entertain.

My parents had endured a lot during the first few years of their marriage. The stares from others, the whispers, the mean and rude comments. My mom was a black woman, and my dad was white. Her family was more accepting of her marring a white man than his family was of him marrying a black woman. It took time, but Dad's family grew to love her. Mom told me once that she loved Dad so much that she wasn't going to allow his family to run her off. She said that showing people kindness and the love of God would soften their hearts. She understood that it was only fear that made his family that way. Fear of not knowing anything about her and her background. My mom showed them that they were all more alike than different.

Funny how my dad's mom lives with us now. My grandmother ended up depending on my mom to do so much for her when she moved in a few years ago. Mom was just so nice to everyone—why did this happen to her? After we talked, Dad left the room and headed back downstairs.

"Hey, San! Your dad said I could find you in his room on the chaise. Can I sit with you for a few? We don't have to talk if you don't want."

Hannah was a sweetie, she never wanted to get in the way or be a burden. I needed a friend to talk to, and she was always the perfect one for me to call on.

"Hi, Hannah! Please sit. Did you like the service today?"

"Yes. It was a beautiful celebration of your mother's life!"

"I thought so also, and Mom did a great job planning everything. I will really miss her and that beautiful smile."

"She did have a beautiful smile, and so many other assets that you can always hold on to."

"Hannah, I have to confess to someone about a sin of mine."

"You don't have to confess to me—do you want to pray about it?"

"No, I need to get this out, and I need you to be honest with me. Hannah, I think I was embarrassed of my mom. That is probably why I was so mean to her."

"Oh, Cassandra, your mom had been through a serious sickness. She lost so much weight, she became weak, and she tried to keep up with you, but it became hard. No reason to think that you were embarrassed of her. You tried to tell her to stay home several times to get rest and not come to your events; you understood her sickness, and so did she."

"No, no! I was embarrassed of her skin color! I hate myself for even saying that, but it is true! She was darker than me, and I treated her so badly for it. When I was younger, I would ask her on several occasions if she could bleach her skin so that she could look as light as me and Daddy. I was awful to her, yet she loved me regardless. All she wanted to do was to spend time with me and have mother and daughter time. It was when I was sixteen years old that I finally started looking at her like a mother and not a maid—that was just a year ago! I was short with my responses when talking to her. I would reject her calls when I was out with friends. I would give my dad a hug and kiss goodnight, and just tell her goodnight with a high-five as I walked away. She would just laugh and say, "I understand; you are a daddy's girl." I just had no connection, or didn't want one, because she was a black woman. I look like a white girl with a golden tan, and I could not see her as my mom. I saw her cry and pray regarding me all the time. It feels like God took her away from me because I didn't love her like a daughter should love a mother. She was a beautiful gift given to me that I did not accept, and I am now realizing how much she really meant to me. The pain and hurt I caused her over the years seem worse than her having cancer. I am her child that she gave birth to—how could I not love her unconditionally?"

"Oh, San! Your mom knew you loved her. A mother's love is unconditional; they love us regardless of…"

"Please don't make excuses for me. I only really showed her love within the last year. I wasted so much time being arrogant, nasty, and a brat toward her. I don't think I can ever forgive myself for this. Hannah, I think I need to be alone. It has been a long day, and I need to get some rest."

"I understand. Everyone has gone home. It was just a few of us here helping your dad and grandma clean up downstairs. Just remember that I am a call away, day or night. I love you, San, and God loves you more. There is nothing too hard for God to fix. I know your mom is gone, but she knew you loved her, and she only wanted and prayed for the best concerning you."

"Have a good night, Hannah, and tell your family thanks for attending today."

I was not trying to hear all that about anyone loving me. I just wanted to die. I was just afraid that I would not end up with my mom in heaven, since she was much nicer than me. I began to stare at the ceiling for a while, then I closed my eyes and cried myself to sleep.

GOODBYE

CHAPTER 12

"Good morning, Dad—I slept all night in Mom's chaise again."

"I know, and I didn't want to wake you. You looked so peaceful, I just wanted you to get as much rest as possible."

"Thank you! How are you doing this morning, Dad?"

"I am doing good! The service was so beautiful yesterday that you could feel her presence—and most importantly, the peace of God was in the place. It was everything your mom wanted. I was sad, but very happy at the same time. How are you doing this morning?"

"I really miss her, Dad! I just wish we had more time to be together, so that I could tell her how awesome she is… I mean was, as a mother."

"I know, pumpkin! I have something on your bed from your mom. She wanted me to give it to you the morning after the service; it was her wish. When you go to your room, take some time, and when you are done, I will be downstairs making breakfast."

Before Dad could finish talking, I was in my room sitting on my bed. It was a pink floral envelope addressed to me, Ms. Cassandra Davis, Mommy's Baby Girl. The letter was written on beautiful, pink floral stationary that matched the envelope.

I made sure to open it without tearing the envelope, but thankfully it was not sealed. Mom's cursive writing was so beautiful. She was a third-grade teacher, and she got a lot of practice. She was always teaching her students how to write in cursive.

My heart began to beat fast as I imagined my mom talking to me when reading the letter:

My beautiful and sweet Cassandra! I love you more than you can ever know! When you have children one day, you will understand the love that a mother has for her child. The love that I feel for you is from God. When I gave birth to you, it was magical when we finally met. I was the most blessed woman that day. I thought I couldn't have children, but God blessed me with you. You were perfect! Perfect to hold, perfect to touch, just a perfect gift from above! Your dad and I adored you! When we finally made it home, we would stare at you all night! We were in awe of how God's creation was so perfect. The love your dad and I have for each other is an example of God's perfect love. All we ever wanted to do was share His love with you and with others.

Now that I am gone, I am resting well. I am with my heavenly Father, so don't cry or be sad. You were a great daughter! I know you didn't understand a lot when you were growing up, and as you became a teen, you were still trying to figure it out. Just remember that you are strong, intelligent, and an independent young woman who will be used by God. He has an amazing plan for your life. I have trained you in more ways than you can even imagine, and I know God will perfect those ways over the years. You will have good days and bad days, and even sad days. Just allow my spirit to live in you. That would be my smile, my kindness, my compassion, and most importantly, my love. With my spirit in you and your incredible willpower, you will be able to carry on with God on your side, because He lives in you like He did me. It is His Spirit that is in charge, if you allow Him to reign in you. I look forward to the day when we are all back together again, but until then, keep God first by praying and showing His love toward others. God will guide and lead you, if you ask Him to. He created you and will never leave or forsake you, regardless of how unworthy you feel. He sees the good in you, like I did!

I love you, my dear! Stay sweet, and know that I have never been prouder of my sweet Baby Girl!

With all my love,
Mom

I sat on my bed for the next hour, crying as I read the letter over and over again. The next thing I knew, my dad was in my room waking me up. He sat next to me. He asked if I wanted breakfast, and I told him I wasn't hungry. He reminded me that I had to eat. I told him that I would get something later, but I just wanted to read the letter and smell Mom's blanket, which I had brought back to my room with me. We talked for the next hour about when I was a little girl, and Dad told really cute stories that Mom had shared with me before. It was good to hear them again. I realized that she was an encourager to so many. Her students loved her, her friends adored her, and she was very active in our church. She had strength that I didn't know existed. All I cared about was hanging out with my friends and preparing for the next school play, but Mom was always there, volunteering and assisting where needed, so that our theater teachers could have smooth productions. She was an angel on earth. Too bad I was seeing it after she was gone.

Dad and I continued to talk. I told him that I wanted to go spend time with Nana later in the summer. Nana was my mom's mother. I told Nana at the funeral that I would spend a week with her within the next few weeks. We both agreed that I would have to get used to my new normal before I went to visit. Nana lived four hours away with her youngest sister, and she expressed how she really missed seeing me. She was super excited that I was coming to see her. Dad agreed that visiting would be good for me; he and Mom had talked about me spending more time with Nana before I went to college. Mom thought that if anyone could give me a good foundation spiritually, it would be my Nana. He also guaranteed me that he and Grandma would be okay, and he even encouraged me to stay longer if I wanted.

Dad and I hugged; he kissed me on my forehead, and he told me that it would take time, and that every day would be a new day that we would have to work on together now that Mom was gone. He also told me that everyone who knew us had been praying for our family, and that in time, we would be okay. Dad went to check on Grandma, and I decided to drink my bottled water that was unopened on my nightstand. I told Dad that I was going to take a shower and come downstairs to sit with Grandma while he worked on boxing up Mom's clothes. I told Dad that I admired him for being so strong, and that I was glad he was my dad. He smiled and said, "Pumpkin, I'm glad you are my daughter. Now take a shower and go get a little something to eat." We both smiled, and I took a shower; I checked on Grandma and talked to her for a while, but I found myself back in my room, lying on my bed, reading and reciting my letter that my angel had left me.

HERITAGE

CHAPTER 13

Since school was out, Mrs. Myers told Dad that Grandma staying with her and her family for a few weeks could be good for us all, while he continued to clean out Mom's things. I was also going to go visit Nana. We all agreed that Dad having an entire week alone could help him with his grieving process.

I kissed Dad and Grandma goodbye and headed to my Nana's house. I was so surprised that Dad had allowed me to drive four hours away without him, even though I had done it before. He said he needed to allow me to continue to grow into my independent self, and especially with my senior year starting soon, he wanted me to get used to driving more than two hours away. As I was driving, it felt as if he was sitting next to me. Dad called me every thirty minutes. I left Saturday morning at 8:00 a.m. so that I could arrive by lunch time. It was peaceful and very calm as I drove. Although Dad called me nonstop, it was refreshing to hear his voice. I knew he loved me, and was my protector, but I needed him to calm down.

I arrived at Nana's cute yellow three-bedroom patio home. The flowers in her flowerbed were so pretty in front of her house that I sat outside gazing at them. The beautiful arrangements were like therapy to me, with all the pretty colors. They reminded me of heaven's flowers that my mom would always talk about in her dreams. They were the most beautiful flowers I had seen on earth.

Being with Nana was like being with Mom! We cooked, cleaned, and looked at photo albums until midnight every night. Without much technology in Nana's home, looking at photos was her way of entertaining. When my mom was younger, her family took pictures all the time. Nana had a new photo album we looked at each night, and she had to explain each picture in great detail. We laughed, cried, and laughed harder at each picture every time. I never thought I would have so much fun with Nana and my Great Aunt Jean. I didn't realize I had so many family members who lived all over the world. It was like having a virtual family reunion, but with a photo album instead of with family to touch and talk to. The photo albums were as thick as the old dictionary that sat on the bookshelf in Nana's living room. I learned so much about my mom, and even myself. I must admit, I have a really amazing family history, and I enjoyed every moment of it.

My last night, I helped Nana and Aunt Jean clean the kitchen. They had a few family members come over to their house after church on Sunday, and we had a feast. I saw several aunts, uncles, and cousins who were at the funeral. Everyone was so nice, and super funny. I didn't know we had so many comedians in the family. Everyone had a joke to tell, and we all laughed. I guess laughing is good for the soul, as the old folks say a lot. My mom would tell me and Dad that all the time.

I couldn't believe that a week had gone by so fast! I was very sad to be leaving in the morning. I wished I could stay the entire summer—being with Nana made me feel safe, loved, and protected, as if I was still a little girl, but I couldn't think of leaving my dad by himself. My mom was his everything, and I knew he was missing me. He called me twice a day. He called in the morning to say have a good day, and at night to hear about my day. I would review my day with him and all the events that took place. He loved the stories I shared with him, and he would laugh as if he was here with me. He sounded sad, and kind of pathetic, on the phone. I felt sorry for him, and me. Being on the phone with Dad reminded me of our loss.

I kissed Aunt Jean goodnight; she said she was going to bed because the midnight photo album reviews had her exhausted, plus she wanted to see me off the next morning and could not oversleep. This gave me and Nana time to really talk. She asked me how I was doing. As soon as she asked that question, I threw myself in her arms and cried like a baby. She was so soft and cuddly. At that moment, I really enjoyed her being my Nana. I missed my mom so much that having Nana gave me comfort, especially knowing that she had raised my mom.

"To know that I will never see Mom again hurts so bad! She will not be here for my graduation, when I get married, or even when I have my first child. I miss her so much, Nana."

"I know, my child! I miss her too! She was my firstborn, and I never thought I would outlive any of my kids, but I did. We must pray to our heavenly Father when we get sad and start missing her. We will see her again, but we must believe and have faith that God will help us when we begin to feel sad. You can also read one of her favorite scriptures in the Bible, or read a book that she enjoyed, or listen to music that would relax her. For our emotional strength, we must set our hopes on things above, which is our heavenly Father and all that He promised us if we seek His kingdom to get through this. We can seek God by praying, reading the Bible, and reading Christian material that He has blessed authors to write for us. Books that help us with hope, that give us inspiration and encouragement."

We sat and held each other for what seemed like an eternity. Nana continued with, "Your mom asked me to give you this photo album of her growing up and going through all of the memories you just mentioned. She prayed over this album, with hopes that if you had a question, you could look at the pictures and her inscriptions, and you would know what to do if the need arose. Don't worry, Baby Girl! God always has a ram in the bush. He will give you what you need when you need it, and especially if you ask Him for it. Your mom and I actually put this together for you. It was our final project that we worked on together. It is very meaningful to us both, because we know it will be helpful to you."

I had no words, except: "Thank you, Nana!" I sat on the couch next to her and continued to cry as I turned each page that was filled with pictures, cards, letters, memories, and joy, from my mom's childhood through my junior year in high school. This album was priceless and very special to me. I planned to keep adding to the photo album and to pass it along to my children.

We finally kissed each other and headed to bed. I called Dad and told him about my day, and expressed how special this trip had been for me. I told him that I had learned so much about me, my mom, and her family. I was able to look at everyone differently. I was able to see my mom through everyone. Her beliefs, her values, and her perspective on life were all part of her experiences and how she was raised. I now understood where her loving nature and strong belief in God came from—it came from a strong family.

APPRECIATIVE

CHAPTER 14

I pulled away from Nana's house at 11:00 a.m. It was difficult getting out of bed, since she and I had sat up until midnight each night talking and reminiscing. Nana made me an awesome breakfast. Everything was from scratch. Who does that these days? I had learned so much, even how to cook, which was going to blow my dad's mind. I waved at Nana and Aunt Jean as I pulled away. I was so glad they had each other, since they were both widows. Nana cried as I waved goodbye, and we promised each other that we would talk a few times every week. Nana also made my dad promise that we would all come to visit for Thanksgiving dinner and stay the entire week with her—she even wanted Grandma to join us. Nana said it would be a great trip for everyone. That would be too long for me; I would have to return during the summer, Memorial Day weekend, and any other holiday or break, even if it was by myself.

My four hours went fast as I drove home. I pulled into the driveway, and I was happy to see Dad and Grandma, but it didn't feel like home anymore to me. It had been a month since Mom had been gone. Being with Nana was like medicine for me and for her. I reminded her of the daughter who had died too soon, and she reminded me of the mother that I didn't get to really know, so we had found comfort in loving Mom through each other.

As I walked into the house, I saw Grandma. I gave her a big hug and kiss. She was so sweet. She had made me some cookies. I got on to her for standing in the kitchen trying to bake, because she used a walker to guide her, but she insisted on having a sweet treat to welcome me back home. Dad ran into the kitchen and greeted me. He was so happy I had arrived safely and had driven through traffic with no problems. I sat and shared my week-long journey that I had with Nana and Aunt Jean. I even pulled out my photo album that Mom and Nana had put together for me. Dad said he would look at it later, because he had to get back to work, so Grandma and I looked at it for hours. When Dad arrived home, he returned with Chinese food—it didn't taste like Nana's southern greens, but it satisfied my hunger. I was just grateful for all of my family!

After dinner, I headed to my room to shower and prepare for bed. I called Nana and thanked her for allowing me time to heal, and for the southern hospitality she and Aunt Jean had showered me with. We both expressed our love for each other and then hung up the phone. I read Mom's letter before I went to bed, cried as I always did, and tried to fall asleep, but I couldn't. I thought and pondered about how I had acted nothing like my mom when she was a teen. I was short-tempered, arrogant, and I acted like people owed me something. As I thought about my life to this point, I realized that I was a spoiled, privileged brat. How could my mother love such a mean-spirited child?

SUPERWOMAN

CHAPTER 15

"Cassandra, Grandma and I are leaving for her doctor's appointment. I am going to let you sleep in. We will be back later this evening, after making some other stops."

"Yes, sir, thanks for telling me. I couldn't sleep. I was up until 5:00 a.m."

"It must have been all the excitement with traveling back home. You will get back on track soon. Stay in bed, and please get some rest! Love you!"

"I love you too, Dad, have a good day!"

As Dad walked away, I knew why I couldn't sleep. I had realized that I was this awful person after seeing how my Nana, my Aunt Jean, and my other relatives on Mom's side were so happy with being family—they didn't have much, shared with everyone they knew, and had joy just celebrating life and each other. I had never seen anything like it. I mean, I had a good life. We traveled, I was very involved in theater at school, I had lots of friends, but it was different at Nana's house. Mom had loved to entertain and host parties and different events. I guess she got it from Nana, but I had never experienced anything like it.

As I lay in the bed, I thought I would try to be a better me. I got up, cleaned the house, washed all the dishes, and washed everyone's clothes. I felt totally exhausted as I returned to the kitchen to check on the Italian spaghetti I had made.

Had I lost my mind? This was too much for one person to do. I was so glad that it was our spring break and the end of April. My school was only open after spring break for two weeks to have teachers review with us, and then we took final exams. When COVID hit a few years ago, our school system decided to end school two weeks after spring break for health reasons. We had been doing this now for three years, since I was a freshman, after the first COVID outbreak. It worked for me, but it seemed that the teachers laid on the work like we were medical students... it was too much, and very overwhelming. I didn't think the teachers realized we had more than one class to study for. My dad said it was because we were high school students, and they were required to get us all college ready, regardless of whether we attended college or not. Then I realized I needed to begin studying, so it wouldn't all hit me at one time... OMG!

Hannah stopped by as I was fixing dinner. I was happy to see her; she and I had only been talking on the phone lately. I gave her a big hug, and she ate some of my spaghetti I had made. I told her about my trip and then showed her my photo album that Mom and Nana had put together for me. As I handed it to her, she noticed cuts on my thigh.

"San, what happened to your inner thigh?"

"Oh, Hannah—nothing, girly! I must have done this at Nana's. I was always helping around the house. I put on these tiny shorts today so that I could clean up for Dad and Grandma, and I forgot all about these marks."

I knew I had just lied to my best friend. I had started cutting at Nana's. Every time I had learned more special things about my mom, it destroyed me, simply because I realized she was so special. She was this outgoing, talented, and kind individual that had loved me so much, and I didn't feel that I gave much love back in return. All I ever did was complain, and talk about me and what I wanted and needed, not realizing that my mom was dying right before my own eyes.

"If you say so, but San—they look like fresh cut marks. Have you been cutting on yourself?"

She had called me out, and I didn't know what to say. Should I continue to lie? She was my best friend and had worse dirt on me then this, so I came clean.

"Yes, but I was only trying it to see how it would feel. When I did it the first time, it did hurt at first, but it seems to make me feel better, I guess. I guess I have been missing Mom more than I thought; her not being with us really hurts."

"Oh, San, you will always miss her, and the pain will be there, but it is important to find other ways to deal with the pain you are feeling. You can't take out on your body what life has taken from you. Self-harm is not the way to go; it can become addictive."

"Hannah, you sound so much like your mom right now. I will not become an addict over this. It was only a few times, and then I stopped. I tried to hide it from Nana; I didn't want to upset her. Besides, each day at her home was like medicine—I actually found therapy in just being with Nana, since she reminded me so much of Mom."

"Well, that is good to know. However, I heard that if you use ice to numb an area of your body like where you have cut, it can actually help as you continue to heal. You are a beautiful girl, and nothing is worth you harming yourself."

As Hannah finished talking, Dad and Grandma walked into the house. Hanna gave me a hug and said she would see me at school tomorrow. Dad and Grandma were so impressed with the house and the dinner that I had prepared that they talked about it all night.

I spent the night in my room, preparing for my final exams and thinking about what Hannah had said to me. As the night continued, I realized that it was 3:00 a.m., and that I was not tired. I tried to lie down and force myself to sleep, but it didn't happen. I decided to read Mom's letter and look through my photo album, but still no sleep. It was now 6:00 a.m., so I decided to begin getting ready for school, but I had to cook breakfast for Dad and Grandma first. It made me happy to see them happy when I helped around the house.

I left a note on the kitchen table for them with the breakfast I had made, telling them to have a great day! Then I headed to school.

DENIAL

CHAPTER 16

The week of finals went well. Even though I had only slept five hours for the entire two weeks since being back home, I was not sleepy. I tried to tire myself out with hopes of being sleepy by bedtime. I prepared breakfast daily, and I even cooked dinner, so that Dad could focus on Grandma and his own work. The washing of clothes was not for me. I hated folding them, so I told everyone they were on their own for clean clothes. My dad thought my comment was so funny that he laughed for hours. I didn't get it!

Hannah called and asked me if I wanted to hang out with a few other friends to celebrate the end of another school year, but I wanted to stay home and clean, and order takeout for the family. I also wanted to read my mom's letter and look at the photo album she gave me. My friends didn't understand how it was to have your mom die right before your very eyes. Regardless of whether they lived with both parents or not, at least they had a mom to go home to. Plus, I wasn't in the mood! I wasn't feeling energetic, and I didn't want to hang. I wanted to see my mom and talk to her. I told Hannah that I had made plans with my dad. Hannah paused on the phone as if she was concerned, and asked me if I was really okay. I told her I was, and to go hang out, because all I really wanted to do was stay home with Dad and Grandma.

We had a good time. We ordered pizza and watched a movie about a dog trying to find his way back home to his owners. It was sad, but it had a good storyline. It was midnight, and we all decided that it was time for bed. As I headed to my room, Dad asked me how everything was going. I told him I was okay, but that I was still missing Mom more every day. I also shared with him that I couldn't sleep. He looked concerned. He said that he would call my doctor and make an appointment. We talked a little more, and he even shared with me how he still missed Mom and that we would always miss her, but that it was important for us to balance our day out and stay busy. He gave me some suggestions and even asked if I wanted therapy to help with my grief. I said no, and that I could handle it. Dad kissed me on my forehead, and we both headed to our rooms.

As I sat on my bed, I started to cry yet again. I had cried every night since my mom's death, and it would not stop. I thought about the ice Hannah had mentioned when I felt the urge to cut, but I didn't feel like walking down the stairs to the kitchen. I looked around my room, found a sharp object, and I did it again. I felt a sense of calmness, but not sleep. I remembered that my Dad had some sleeping pills that his doctor had prescribed for him, because he wasn't sleeping when Mom was in her last stage of cancer, and he couldn't sleep after her death. He took the pills for about two weeks, then he stopped after he felt like himself again. I headed to his bathroom, looked in the cabinet where he kept his medicine, grabbed the pills, and headed back to my room. I needed some sleep, so I took about eight of them. I guess I should have read the instructions before I took them. When I did, it read:

Dangerous! Do not exceed more than two pills a day and do not have with other medication! As I kept reading, I realized that they were not sleeping pills. As I kept reading the directions, I saw that they were for anxiety! The meds had been in my system for about ten minutes, and I was starting to feel a little strange and sick to my stomach. I ran to Dad, woke him up, and told him what I had done, thinking they were sleeping pills—especially since I'd had some cold medicine three hours prior. He looked at me with fear, and as he tried to catch me, he said, "Cassandra, your legs are bleeding!"

All I remembered was him calling an ambulance as I fell over on his bed, feeling extremely sleepy and sick to my stomach.

Life's Reality

CHAPTER 17

"Hannah, this is your last weekend before your senior year begins on Wednesday! Five more days! I know you are excited! Oh, by the way, you should invite your friends to the youth celebration at the Civic Center on Saturday. It has been the talk of the town."

"Mom, it has been the talk of the town for you and your friends for months!" We both laughed as Mom was making her morning coffee before heading to work. She said she was going to have a very busy Friday, like she does every year before the first few days of school. However, she went on and on about Saturday's event.

"Mom, everyone knows about the Back-to-School Youth Explosion tomorrow. I plan on meeting the yearbook staff there before it begins to take some photos. San and I have also decided to drive over together. Some of the kids just want to attend for the outside barbecue, the relay games, and all the free back-to-school giveaways, while others plan on attending to hear the guest speakers and the musical entertainment."

"Well, honey, regardless of why anyone wants to attend, the fact that they attend is all that matters. The food, the games, the goodies, and the music are ways to attract the attention of all of you youth. The message that will go forth by the guest speakers will be amazing, and it could really help someone with their salvation and spiritual walk with Jesus! I am just hoping that students show up. I can tell you one thing: Pastor Ronnie is beside himself with pure joy that our church is hosting this event! Make sure that you send some reminders to your friends, especially to Steven and his friends."

"Yes, I will text him." I wasn't the most enthusiastic when she said Steven's name. He had finally texted me when he returned from partying at the beach with some of his football friends. He had claimed they were there to work on some throwing drills. Well, I heard that a few girls met them, and they worked on more than drills. The sand drills made it into the pool—as well as into his beach house—while I was home in the bed, crying my eyes into a swollen mess. Steven told me he had stayed to himself, and his friends were the ones having the party; he claimed he was just there to provide the house. All I could say to him was, "Whatever!" He and I hadn't really talked much. It was awkward every time he called me, so we had only been texting each other.

Mom kissed me and headed out the door for a day of fun. She loved her job; she just disliked all the work and constant paperwork that schools gave them and the teachers, especially since COVID a few years ago. As Mom walked away, she waved as if I was the mom and she was my daughter, going away on a long trip. I laughed and thought, *Eight hours will be here in no time,* so I shouted, "Have a great day, Mom!"

I did what my mom asked of me, and texted him: "Hey, BTW Mom wants U 2 attend tomorrow's back 2 school celebration. I know several sports teams, clubs, and youth groups from several schools and churches will be there. I just wanted U 2 know."

CHAPTER 18

"Hannah, I am having so much fun! This has been such a fun day! So glad your pastor did this for the youth in our community. The food was delicious, the games were fun, and the giveaways were not cheap. Even your parents and my dad are having fun serving all the students in different individual events."

"Yeah—I think our parents were just being nosey while watching us have fun, especially when we were in the relay race. I can't believe you lost your right shoe and you didn't stop! You are so hilarious, San—that was very funny!" We laughed as we cooled our bodies off with a bottle of water and watched others enter the stadium. Everyone was given a mask to wear at the entrance and asked to sanitize before entering the arena.

The numbers of COVID had gone down. It had been a few years since we were hit with the worst of it, but large events like this still caused everyone to be extra careful.

All the participants were taking a seat to cool down from all the food, games, and giveaways. We sat in our seats drinking our water as we watched the different performers sing Christian gospel, gospel rap, and some inspirational pop and R & B songs. I felt as if I were at a big party. It was good to see so many students singing out loud to the songs and moving to the beat of the music. The masks on their faces did not stop them from singing. There were even some kids dancing to the gospel music that was playing. It was like being at a real concert—I guess we were entertaining and praising Jesus, even if we didn't know we were.

As I continued to scan the atmosphere, I could see hundreds of students having such a good time. I even saw Allen, my friend who has said he doesn't believe in God. He was laughing and throwing a beach ball around with a few of his friends. It was nice to see him having fun from a distance. I could see a few of our yearbook photographers walking around and taking pictures in the arena as we waited for the guest speakers to take the stage.

It was awesome in the arena. Balloons and beach balls were being thrown around as everyone was laughing and enjoying the music. No parents, except the event folks standing by the entrances, and all of us teens. The parents who were helping were cleaning up outside. As I continued to look around, I saw him. He was sitting two rows behind me. My heart started beating faster than normal, and my stomach began to feel very nauseated. San saw him and his friend Matthew at the same time I did.

She shouted, "Look, Hannah, there are Steven and Matt! Guys, come and sit by us!"

Before I could stop her, Steven and Matthew were in the front row with us. I told San not to move down and that I was comfortable in my seat. I pointed to the two empty chairs six feet away, on the other side of her. Matthew sat close to San and Steven sat next to him. San gave me a look and asked what was going on. I told her nothing and to chill with the questions. I reminded her that I was having a great day and said that seeing him was making my skin crawl.

San was shocked at how I was acting toward Steven. She just looked at me and started laughing. She had never witnessed me getting so upset with Steven. However, before she could say another word, the lights began to dim and the music changed. It was time—it was time to hear our guest speakers, and I was happy that they entered the stage at that moment.

CHAPTER 19

"Hello, everyone! I hope and pray that everyone has had a remarkable day so far! The food, the games, and the giveaways were just what we all needed. I also saw you all on camera dancing while we were in the back, and I became jealous because I wanted to get out here and get my dance on with you! This is my kind of party!" Everyone inside the arena erupted with screams and laughter as the beach balls continued flying high in the air from person to person when he mentioned dancing.

He went on to say, "My name is Minister Mike Kemp, but please call me Minister M, and this is my beautiful wife standing next to me, Minister Mimi, and you can also call her Minister M. I guarantee you that one of us will answer. We are Ministers M & M." We all laughed.

"We are the youth pastors at our church in California. We came here today to join you in your back-to-school festivities in the beautiful state of Alabama, where we have been greeted with southern hospitality since we got off the plane. We would like to send out a special thank you to Pastor Ronnie Banks and his spiritual team for loving on us. There is no greater love than to show the love of Christ one to another, so we say thank you, Pastor Ronnie. We are also here to have what we call a Back-to-School Encouragement Chat. With that being said, thank the person next to you with an elbow bump for gracing us with their presence today. Now turn and elbow the other person that is sitting on the opposite side—if no one is on that side, elbow yourself... give yourself some of that Godly love!" Everyone laughed while looking around to see who was elbowing themselves.

"If you have a cell phone, take it out and send a Snapchat message, or some form of communication, to your friends and family about today's celebration. If you do not have a cell phone, bother the person next to you and ask to use theirs—and yes, keep those masks on while doing it." He paused as everyone, and I mean everyone, took out their cell phone to Snapchat, tweet, text, or do what we love to do as teens. Some were also taking group pictures and selfies.

San and I hugged while trying to take a picture together with our cell phones, until Steven and Matthew ran behind us to photo bomb it. I must admit, the energy in the place was crazy exciting. We were all having a lot of fun.

"You all are awesome at following directions! If your teachers could see you now." Ministers M & M both laughed with everyone. San and I thought Minister Mike seemed full of life and fun to listen to.

Minister Mike continued with, "Now hold your cell phone up and look at it. Yes, that is what I said: look at it. That is why we flew all these miles, because we want to see you look at your cell phones. Seriously, though, think about this: why do we have a cell phone, and what is its purpose?"

As several students began to shout out why they had a cell phone, Minister M went on to say, "Yes, cell phones are very important to many of us. You need them for emergencies, for parents to keep up with you—especially if you are drivers, and even if you walk to and from school, they just want to make sure you are safe and have made it to your destination. Cell phones are also helpful when you go to college, or when some of you need to text home during the week that you are sick, even before stepping foot in the school nurse's office. Some of you use your cell phones to text mom or dad and tell them that the teacher did you wrong, because you got a bad grade on a test at school or a project that they helped you with or did for you." Everyone began talking and laughing and even giving high fives, as if they were reminiscing about the time when that happened.

"A lot of us use cell phones for entertainment and social-ization. We talk, text, tweet, Facetime, Snapchat, TikTok, play games, pay bills, surf the internet, make appointments, watch movies, take pictures, put together videos, order food—you name it, we do it! Having a cell phone can also help you show your maturity to your parents by not abusing your usage. Cell phones have become vital to us all.

"Having a cell phone is like a way to escape. We even get upset if someone, especially our parents, threatens to take our cell phones away due to bad grades and not focusing in school, or even doing something they feel is morally wrong or life-threatening while on the phone. Sometimes, we lose the phone on our own. If we can't find our phone, we think the world has come to an end until we find our cell phone. We can't think, we can barely sleep, we even zone others out while we are searching for our cell phone.

"We treat our cell phone as if it is human. So, think about it: if our phone is that special to us, how do we protect it? Please stay with me, everyone—I promise I am going somewhere with this." Minster M had more shouts regarding how to protect a cell phone.

"We can do so many things to protect or not protect our cell phone. We want to make sure our phones are not in the sun too long, because they can overheat, or if cell phones are outside in freezing weather they could freeze. Some of us like to place our cell phones in our pockets, in purses or bookbags, and in other places that one can only ask: why are you doing that? Having a cell phone is cool, but we need to learn how to take care of them.

"However, you all are correct! We protect our cell phone with a screen protector, and a cell phone case for even more protection, so that the body of the phone is protected. Kind of like wearing these masks over our nose and mouth. We wear the mask to protect. When it comes to our cell phones, who wants scratches and dust particles in and around their cell phone? Most importantly, who wants a *Broken* or shattered cell phone screen? *Broken*—that is what my wife and I want to talk to you all about." Minister Mike then passed his wife the microphone.

"Minister Mike just gave us all some things to think about. He asked us why we have a cell phone, and we all agreed that we really need our phones. He then asked us how we protect the cell phone we own."

Everyone in the arena was listening. I couldn't believe they had gotten our attention by talking about cell phones. As I scanned the room again, everyone seemed intrigued. I had a feeling that this would change from being about our cell phones to being more about us, and boy was I correct. Minister MiMi continued with, "We want you all to now look at your cell phone one more time. Look at your cell phone as if it is a representation of you. You are the cell phone. What is your purpose? Are you important? Why are you here? How do you protect yourself? How many scratches and cracks do you have from life? Or are you *Broken*?"

I felt my heart sink when she said the word *Broken*. I looked over at San, who had tears streaming down her face. When I looked past her, I could see Steven looking at me; then he turned his head back toward the guest ministers when our eyes met. All I could do was close my eyes and inhale and exhale. Then I began to tear up. I realized that, just like a cell phone that has fallen, I now had scratches because of not having a strong screen protector. I too was *Broken*.

CHAPTER 20

Minister Mimi proceeded to say that prior to visiting our state they had done some research. In their research they were able to see the percentage of students who had attempted suicide because they were *Broken*. They researched the percentage of students who had abortions because they were *Broken*. They researched the percentage of students who had been to drug rehab because they were *Broken*, and the percent of students who had been in trouble with the law because they were *Broken*.

"What about those of you that we could not do research on? You are being abused and mistreated. You feel alone and isolated. Others have been betrayed and abandoned, and some may feel confused and misunderstood. The shame and embarrassment, peer pressure, and attacks from others all lead to being *Broken*. Even if you have anxiety, depression, worries, and fears, you too may feel *Broken*.

"Some of you may say your parents don't understand you, or your friends are materialistic and into themselves. Others may be crying out that they don't want to go back to school because the teachers don't get their true creativity, or that they are tired of getting in trouble for just being themselves. Some feel alone and rejected by friends who do not want to hang out or associate themselves with them, or maybe some have friends who have moved away. Let's not forget those who had a loved one that passed away. Every one of you may feel *Broken*.

"Some of you did not realize that what you were feeling was brokenness. Well, let me tell you: even though you have been *Broken*, this does not have to be your *life's reality*! Every one of us has been wonderfully made, regardless of what we have done or what others may think about us. God thinks we are awesome, and He has created each of us with a purpose, and we all have a divine plan to fulfill. We are going to put scriptures around the arena on every screen so that everyone in this arena can see and read aloud with me. Let's start with Mark 11:25 in the New International Version of the Bible. The New International Version tells us, 'If you hold anything against anyone, forgive them, so that your Father in heaven may forgive you your sins.' Yes, that is what it says—we must forgive others who have wronged us! That is not always easy, but it is a way to fix some of the brokenness and failures of life that we may be feeling. Before Minister Mike comes back to speak, I want you to turn to someone sitting next to you, but please do not leave anyone out of this conversation. You can have 2–3 in a group. Discuss, for a few minutes, why it is good to forgive others who have wronged and even mistreated you."

As music played softly in the background, everyone turned to someone to discuss why they should forgive others. I wasn't the one to answer that question, but I knew I had to step it up and act like I hadn't gone through anything—San needed me. She needed to talk; she needed to get out how she was feeling. I was sad, because I had experienced a loss also, and I was *Broken*. I still didn't know how to get through it. What Ministers M & M were saying was really good, and I could tell it had reached so many of us in the arena. I was curious as to what they would say next.

San and I talked about how forgiveness would help us with our healing, and how if we didn't forgive others, it would only cause us to continue to be angry, sad, depressed, and even isolated from others in life. It made so much sense that forgiveness is part of the healing process.

As we finished talking, Steven blew me a kiss and motioned with his lips that he was sorry and to please forgive him. I couldn't say anything to him—I only gave him a stare and motioned to him to pull his mask back over his mouth and nose.

CHAPTER 21

"Yes, you are the cell phone! Some of you may have been scratched, cracked, and even shattered, to the point that it has caused you to be *Broken*. This is why you need protection! 'God is our refuge and strength, a very present help in trouble.' You can find that in Psalm 46:1 in the King James Version of the Bible, which I will refer to as the KJV. You can also find in Deuteronomy 31:6 that it says to: 'Be strong and of a good courage, fear not, nor be afraid of them: for the Lord thy God, he it is that doth go with thee; he will not fail thee, nor forsake thee.' In Hebrews 13:6, you get, 'The Lord is my helper, and I will not fear what man shall do unto me.' This leads me to ask you all: is your life perfect? Will you never have disappointments or pain? Life can be hard and can hit you in your heart, where it hurts the most. My question to you all is, why be in this world without protection? Your life's disappointment can be God's appointment of purpose for you! Let God be your covering of protection. Jesus died for our sins so that He could be that covering of protection for us. I want everyone to look at the screen, and let's all read aloud **John 3:16 together. It reads,** 'For God so loved the world, that he gave his only begotten Son, that whosoever believeth in him should not perish, but have everlasting life.' The KJV has every area of hurt, pain, disappointment, sadness, peace, joy, happiness—

109

and I could go on and on about what is covered for us all in the Bible. God left nothing out that we could not read and gain strength from. That is just how much He loves us; all I know is that I want His everlasting life and love.

"In a few minutes, I want you to stand. If I call out something you have been dealing with, you do not have to raise your hand; just listen for now. I will ask you to stand if you can relate to anything I have called out. How many of you are grieving because of losing someone? How many of you have been abusing drugs that may have been or may not have been prescribed to you, or drinking alcohol that you should not be drinking? Which of you are having premarital sex, and you know this is not how God wants you to use your body—you know you should wait until you get married to the one whom God has approved for you. Maybe someone is taking advantage of you and you are too afraid to tell someone. Maybe you are abusing your body in other ways, like cutting yourself to get away from reality and all the pain; or maybe you are not eating properly or on purpose. Maybe you have a foul mouth. Every word you speak is a curse word, or maybe you talk about others to no end, simply because you are unhappy. Maybe you have allowed fear to set up in your heart, and you are allowing doubt, shame, and low self-esteem to grow in you because you believe what has been said to you. How many of you have what you think is a terrible home life? You and your parents do not get along, or maybe they don't have time for you, and you are starting to resent them—some days you don't even like them. Maybe your parents are druggies, and you want them to be parents to you. Some of you may be ashamed of your parents because of their physical appearance, what they do for a living, or for some other reason that causes embarrassment for you. Some of you may live in fear and constant worry, or maybe you don't believe in Jesus Christ our Lord and Savior, but you are willing to give him a try. If I called anything out that you think pertains to you, please stand! No need to look around! Remember, you are the cell phone, and some of these reasons could be why you are *Broken*. Remember, you will not be standing alone."

As the entire arena of students stood, Minister Mike went on to say, "We are not here to judge anyone! Just remember that your neighbor has no clue as to why you are standing! I also need you to believe in your heart that you are standing because this is your moment for healing and restoration. You are standing because you need a spiritual covering, and that covering is Jesus Christ! He is the one who can heal you. It has been His grace and love that has been keeping and protecting you to this point. His protection will continue to protect you. Most importantly, He wants you to accept Him as your Lord and Savior. He wants to help you, heal you, protect you, and guide you. He wants you to walk in your purpose, your destiny. He knows what life has done to you, and He still loves you. He has decided to love you until you can learn to love Him back, and then love you all over again! Just give him a try; He will not lie to you or promise you anything that He cannot provide. He is God and God alone!"

San and I held hands with each other as we stood. Everyone in the arena, in my peripheral vision, was standing, even Steven. I could hear some students sniffing their noses; some were wiping tears from their eyes, while others quietly listened. I knew San was crying. I was numb—I felt nervous, but relief filled my body as theses ministers called students to repentance and healing—even me. We are not perfect, but some think they are. Even though we know we are doing wrong, some of us knowingly keep doing the same thing over and over again. I was no saint, I knew I had been *Broken*; I just wanted to be free again so that I could live.

As Minister Mike gave his wife the microphone, she said, "As you are standing, I want you to know that just like it says in 1 Peter 2:9, you are 'a chosen generation, a royal priesthood, an holy nation, a peculiar people; that ye should shew forth the praises of him who hath called you out of darkness into his marvellous light.' Students, it is important to open your eyes and turn from darkness, which is sin, and turn toward light, which is walking in love, kindness, forgiveness, and obedience. Turn from the power of Satan, and turn unto God, that you may receive forgiveness of your sins. You can read more in Acts 26:18. And to love God with all our heart, and with all our understanding, and with all our soul, and with all our strength, and to love your neighbour as yourself, is more than any offerings and sacrifice, as Mark 12:33 puts it. You must also remember that there is no fear in love, and as 1 John 4:18 states, 'Perfect love casteth out fear: because fear hath torment. He that feareth is not made perfect in love.' God loves you, and He is love!

"I know some of you have been through hell and back. The torment, pain, and agony that some of you may be going through have been awful. However, let God show you how to turn what was meant for evil into good, where it can help someone else. This is what I call the call of God to make a difference! You can be that difference with someone now, or someone in your future that you have not even met yet.

"However, in the King James Version of the Bible, which we will place on the screen and read aloud together, it says in 1 John 1:9, 'If we confess our sins, he is faithful and just to forgive us our sins, and to cleanse us from all unrighteousness.' *He* refers to Jesus. Also, in Matthew 6:14-15, 'For if ye forgive men their trespasses, your heavenly Father will also forgive you: but if ye forgive not men their trespasses, neither will your Father forgive you your trespasses.' James 5:16 goes on to says that we should 'Confess your faults one to another, and pray one for another, that ye may be healed. The effectual fervent prayer of a righteous man availeth much.' I also found in Proverbs 10:12 that 'Hatred stirreth up strifes: but love covereth all sins.'

My point today, students, is that if we confess with our mouth that Jesus is Lord and believe in our hearts that He died for our sins, we can be saved. It clearly says that He will forgive us of our sins and heal us where we are *Broken*. Knowing what you know after reading these scriptures, what do you believe? What do you want in life? Do you want a covering? Do you want to be healed? Take a moment to think about your worst day. How did you get through it? What if Jesus had been your protector on that day that you are thinking about—would the results have been different? Would the outcome have changed? I am not here to have you soak in regret and pity. I just want you to realize that regardless of what you did or said to someone, Jesus still loves you! Jesus has forgiven you, and He wants to give you a brighter and better future. Give Him that opportunity to show you how to give Him glory and honor!

"With no judgment, we want to go into the prayer of salvation together with everyone. Please let your guard down and trust in someone bigger than you; trust in Jesus."

CHAPTER 22

"I would like for us all to pray the prayer of salvation that Minister Mimi and I pray with students as we travel the world. If you have never said this prayer, this will be the day that you become a child of the Most High King, Jesus Christ. If you have said this prayer or one similar, say it again for yourself and along with the person next to you. If you do not want to be a part of what we are doing, you are free to stand or sit, but please do not leave. I pray you will stay and give your life to Jesus Christ, or support the friend that you may be here with. Jesus gave up so much for us. Let us all focus on Christ, so please repeat after me:

"Dear Lord, I come to you just as I am. You know my life and you know how I have been living. Please forgive me, Lord. I repent of my sins. I believe that Jesus Christ is the Son of God, and that Jesus Christ died for my sins. I also believe that on the third day Jesus Christ rose from the dead. Lord Jesus, I ask that you come into my heart, take over my thoughts, and that you live your life in me and through me. I give you permission to be my covering, my source, and my protector forever, in Jesus' name I pray, amen.

"It is that simple—you are now a child of our Lord and Savior Jesus Christ. What do you do now, you may ask? The first thing is: every night and every morning, thank your heavenly Father for your day, for waking you up, for strength, for the talents He has blessed you with, and thank Him for just being the awesome God that He is. God loves the praises of His people. Learn to lift your hands to the heavens and just say thank you. You do not have to always ask Him for something; just learn to praise and worship Him. This is where He will bless you—just try it.

"If you do not have a church home or youth group, it is so important to find a church family where you can grow and learn from. Pastor Ronnie and his youth ministers will be in the lobby after this is over. He will not persuade you to come to his church, but we will invite you. He knows plenty of other churches that may be a great fit for you, where they are teaching truths and not watering down what you can and cannot do. They are preaching what the Bible says. Learn to read good Christian novels, magazines, and other literature, or websites that may be helpful to you.

"Most importantly, talk to Jesus daily, not only in prayer, but like I am talking to you. Tell Him about your day, what went right or wrong. This will help you to develop a relationship with your heavenly Father. He cares about everything you say and do, and He wants to guide you and lead you. That is why He left His Holy Spirit for us all. These are the things you will learn when you join a church or youth group. You owe it to yourself to have the best life that God wants you to have, and that is living and walking in His glory daily and being a living testimony for Him. Let your life be what God has ordained from the beginning. What you have gone through in life will be a blessing and helpful to others—you just need to learn how to make that happen.

"When you leave out of this arena, does this mean that you will have perfect days? No! You may get in an argument with your parents tonight because of something silly, or someone may say something you don't like or agree with. It is up to you to stop, pray to Jesus, and ask for guidance in that moment. Every day is now a day that the enemy will remind you of your past sins, but you have to remember that every scripture we read today is truth. God loves you and cares about you. He has forgiven you and is giving you a fresh start. Starting over just means you are starting over with more experience than the previous day. If you believe that, you will be victorious."

CHAPTER 23

This was the most beautiful thing I had ever witnessed in my life. My classmates saying the repentance prayer, crying, and asking the Lord for forgiveness was awesome! It was such a peaceful, sweet presence in the arena. After most of us said the prayer of salvation together, Minister Mike said the final prayer over us. San and I held each other as we both cried. We proclaimed our salvation together and prayed that we would try our best to be better people for Christ. He does love us and was with us through all that we had experienced in our life. We agreed that we could at least give God more of our time by getting involved with our church youth group, and reading the Bible and inspirational literature to become better servants for Christ. I was just so grateful that God had looked past my sins and decided to love me, regardless of all my faults and wrongdoings.

As the program ended, students lined up to talk to Ministers M & M. They took selfies with them, thanked them, and expressed gratitude for the chat that went forth. San and I sat in our chairs watching all the students hug, cry, and gather around talking, and those who just sat like we did to enjoy the moment. We almost forgot that it was time to go. As we headed to our car after waving bye to the guest speakers, I reminded San that Pastor Ronnie was having a parent panel with the Ministers M

& M on Sunday afternoon, for those in the community who wanted to learn more about what teens deal with in life. We both laughed and said that our parents would be there.

When we exited the arena, everyone was given a bag of M&M's candy with a scripture on it. We could select plain, which represented Mimi's life. She mentioned that she had thought life was too boring and plain, but she finally realized God had made her the person He wanted her to be for a reason, and that her life had turned out very sweet. Or we could choose peanut. Minister Mike said he was a nut growing up, and that he always did nutty things that his parents were always trying to bail him out of. He said he was constantly getting in trouble at school and doing sinful, nutty things all his life, until he gave his life to Christ one day, and the nutty guy he once was turned into a sweet covering of Jesus Christ's love. On both candy bags there was a scripture from Proverbs 3:5-7. San and I agreed that we would save the M&M's bag as a reminder of the night and the encouraging message that would encourage us on those tough days to come. As we walked to my car and discussed the entire day, I saw Steven waiting by my car. San said she would go sit in the car and wait for me while we talked.

"I'm sorry, Hannah! Please forgive me! I have repented tonight, but I still feel a loss, and I know you do. I cannot pray this back. All I can do is continue to pray for you and us. I am praying that we heal from this and can move on. Again, I am sorry, and want you to know that I love you, I love us!"

"Thank you, Steven! This was an amazing day! I was also able to repent. I know God has forgiven us; we just need to learn how to forgive ourselves. It will not be easy, but we must remember His Word. It is us that remembers our sins, not God, after we have repented. That is the kind of God we serve, and I do not ever want to do anything again to harm the body he has given me to serve Him with. I have prayed and thought about this for a few days now, and tonight it was clear to me that we should go our separate ways. I know we will see each other at school, and I want us to be cordial with one another, but I also need to work on me while learning how to have a real relationship with the God who created me. I have lost so much that I cannot give any more out, not at this time in my life. I thank you for being a friend, and I will continue to pray for you also."

"I love you, Hannah, and I pray you heal and do great things in life! You deserve it, and so much more! Have a great senior year!"

Steven walked away. I watched him walk away until I could no longer see him in the dark. He must have parked on the back side of the arena. I sat in the driver's seat of my car with tears flowing down my face. San looked at me and passed me some Kleenex. We did not say a word until I dropped her off at her house.

Before exiting my car, San said, "Hannah, God loves you! Please don't hate yourself for anything that you have done. Just learn how to be the voice for others who may need you in the future, and remember that being *Broken* does not have to stay our reality! I am so glad we experienced this day together. I am about to go call my Nana and tell her all about it! I love you, my BFF, and remember that God loves you more than anyone! I will see you at church in the morning!"

"I love you too, San, and you are right—being *Broken* does not have to stay our reality, because we have a covering, and his name is JESUS!"

ACKNOWLEDGEMENTS

As a high school counselor in education for over twenty years, I want to thank every individual that I have met in my life. I have learned from you, and even from myself, and have many more stories to share. These are stories of strength, encouragement, and endurance, yet to be written. I also am especially thankful for my students. I am thankful that God had our paths cross. I have witnessed pain, joy, and tears from several of you. I will never forget you! Sharing the truth of what many have experienced is how I created *Broken*!

I dedicate *Broken* to all of those students and dear ones who cannot speak truth to those in their inner circle for fear of being judged by those they love.

I also dedicate this book to those who have left memorable memories of love, encouragement, resilience, and tenacity. You touched me, and I thank you for sharing your brokenness—but most importantly, I thank you for helping me realize that being *Broken* is not our *life's reality*!

Proverbs 3:5-7

Trust in the Lord with all thine heart; and lean not unto thine own understanding.
In all thy ways acknowledge him, and he shall direct thy paths.
Be not wise in thine own eyes: fear the Lord, and depart from evil.

With love!
R. D. Smith

SOURCE CITATIONS AND INDEXES

The King James Version – Old Testament
Deuteronomy 3:1-6
Proverbs 3:5-7
Proverbs 10:12
Psalm 46:1

The King James Version – New Testament
Acts 26:8
Hebrews 13:6
James 5:16
John 3:16
1 John 1:9
1 John 4:18
Mark 12:23
Matthew 6:14-15
Philippians 4:13
1 Peter 2:9

The New International Version – New Testament
Mark 11:25

CPSIA information can be obtained
at www.ICGtesting.com
Printed in the USA
BVHW062330220321
603180BV00003B/362